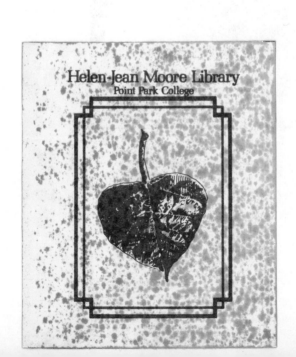

BY JOHN HALL WHEELOCK
The Gardener and Other Poems
Poems Old and New
Poems, 1911–1936
The Bright Doom
The Black Panther
Dust and Light
Love and Liberation
The Belovèd Adventure
The Human Fantasy

SELECTED AND EDITED BY,
WITH INTRODUCTION
Poets of Today VIII
Poets of Today VII
Poets of Today VI
Poets of Today V
Poets of Today IV
Poets of Today III
Poets of Today II
Poets of Today I
Editor to Author: The Letters of
     Maxwell E. Perkins
The Face of a Nation: Poetical Passages
     from the Writings of Thomas Wolfe

IN PREPARATION
Prefaces to Poetry

The Gardener and other poems

THE GARDENER,
and other poems.

John Hall Wheelock

Charles Scribner's Sons
New York

Some of the poems here included were first published in the following periodicals: *The American Scholar, The Atlantic Monthly, The Georgia Review, The Hudson Review, The Kenyon Review, The Lyric, The New Yorker, The New York Herald-Tribune, The New York Times, Poetry: A Magazine of Verse, Poetry Dial, The Saturday Review, The Sewanee Review, Southwest Review, The Times Literary Supplement, The Transatlantic Review, The Virginia Quarterly Review, Voices, The Yale Review.*

The following poems included in this volume appeared originally in *The New Yorker*: "The Gardener" (1957), "The Divine Insect" (omitting stanzas 2, 3, 7, 10 and 17) (1959), the first half of "Anima" under the title "The House in the Green Well" (1961), copyright © 1957, 1959, 1961, The New Yorker Magazine, Inc.

Library of Congress Catalog Card Number: 61-11582

To the memory of my father
William Efner Wheelock

Contents

PART ONE

INTERLUDE

PART TWO

The Gardener and other poems

Part One

The Gardener

Father, whom I knew well for forty years
Yet never knew, I have come to know you now—
In age, make good at last those old arrears.

Though time, that snows the hair and lines the brow,
Has equalled us, it was not time alone
That brought me to the knowledge I here avow.

Some profound divination of your own,
In all the natural effects you sought
Planted a secret that is now made known.

These woodland ways, with your heart's labor bought,
Trees that you nurtured, gardens that you planned,
Surround me here, mute symbols of your thought.

Your meaning beckons me on every hand,
Grave aisles and vistas, in their silence, speak
A language that I now can understand.

In all you did, as in yourself, unique—
Servant of beauty, whom I seek to know,
Discovering here the clue to what I seek.

When down the nave of your great elms I go
That soar their Gothic arches where the sky,
Nevertheless, with all its stars will show,

Or when the moon of summer, riding high,
Spills through the leaves her light from far away,
I feel we share the secret, you and I.

All these you loved and left. We may not stay
Long with the joy our hearts are set upon:
This is a thing that here you tried to say.

The night has fallen; the day's work is done;
Your groves, your lawns, the passion of this place,
Cry out your love of them—but you are gone.

O father, whom I may no more embrace
In childish fervor, but, standing far apart,
Look on your spirit rather than your face,

Time now has touched me also, and my heart
Has learned a sadness that yours earlier knew,
Who labored here, though with the greater art.

The truth is on me now that was with you:
How life is sweet, even its very pain,
The years how fleeting and the days how few.

Truly, your labors have not been in vain;
These woods, these walks, these gardens—everywhere
I look, the glories of your love remain.

Therefore, for you, now beyond praise or prayer,
Before the night falls that shall make us one,
In which neither of us will know or care,

This kiss, father, from him who was your son.

Prayer
(after St. Theresa of Avila)

Have pity on us, Power just and severe,
  Have pity on our greed, our hate, our lust,
And on our unending anxieties, our ugly fear.
  Great Wisdom, grant wisdom to this timid dust.

Have patience with us, who have betrayed one another
  And parted the single and seamless robe of man,
And divided his garments among us, who is our brother.
  Infinite Patience, have patience if You can.

Have mercy on us—because we are merciless
  And have need of mercy we are not worthy of—
And on our angry littleness,
  Pity Inexorable, Remorseless Love.

Complaint of the Indifference of Things

We live in a world that, for the most part,
Doesn't know us. We move as strangers
Among rocks, trees, rivers, mountains,
Unaware that we are here; even the house
We dwell in and are fond of, perhaps,
Has no knowledge of our existence; the rose
Can't tell our touch from the touch of the wind,
And a thousand stars look out and do not see us.
As for other creatures, to most of them,
Except the domesticated ones, of course,
Who regard us, if at all, as magicians
Capable of the best and the worst, we occur
Chiefly as accidents, often unpleasant—
They have excommunicated us
From their society, who are crueller
Even than themselves, they are no longer
On speaking terms with us, we can't
Come very close to any wild thing;
The wren that builds in the eaves of our dwelling
Knows of us only as probable menace,
As possible beneficence; and the ant,
Whose counties we take in our stride, and whose townships
We level with a step, has never heard of us,
Or, if he has, it is no more
Than our own dim sense of the unknown beings
Who bestride us here, as we the ant,
Or move among us invisible
And merciful as the best of us sometimes are

When we sidestep the ant-hill, ruthless
As the best of us sometimes have to be when the tragic
Nature of things makes it necessary.
There is something wistful in our attitude
Toward things—the beautiful indifference
Of mountains or of a flower. The conscious
Desires, and is envious of,
The unconscious: man envies the rock
Its strength, its self-sufficient calm
Outwardly at least, though it represents
The locked fury of billions of atoms—
He moves, lonely and a stranger, among
The things that surround him, with which to fall in love
Is like courting a woman who is asleep.
Oh, almost everything seems to be asleep,
And cannot respond: the rose will not answer,
Nor the earth reply to her lover, the moon
Is unmindful of the poet who addresses her.
Head over heels in love, we dwell
Among beautiful things, like outcasts,
Even while they abide in us,
Who have won them into ourselves and by a supreme
Act of love and faith given them
Another dimension, engendering on them,
Through the embrace of matter by spirit,
The divine reality born of this fusion,
So that they become other than they were:
The moon that shines in your consciousness
Is more than mere mass and luminous contour,
And the rhythm of the surf along the shore

More than mere water in motion, something
Important has been created through the embrace
Of matter by spirit. But, oh, how cold,
How indifferent, is the response of that partner
To our burning love! I have sometimes thought
That the steady immersion of matter in spirit,
Throughout the ages, its being dipped
Again and again in the quivering, fleeting
Film of consciousness that overlies
The turning planet must, in time,
So saturate matter as to infect it
With spirit itself, and thus evoke,
In flower and tree, in wind and water,
The response for which we long; I have thought
That the brilliant sphere that out of dark heaven
Stares into a human mind
Might almost in that mirror discover
Itself, in wonder, there—a star,
Become so at last through fusion with spirit,
Which, by a depth of love that is
Adoring perception, fulfills an otherwise
Unfulfilled creation. Nevertheless,
We have not roused nature from that sleep of hers—
Things remain things, we remain
Their lovers still, and wistfully
Dwell among them, who deeply abide in us,
Yet are ignorant of our presence here,
And will not know it when we are gone.

Direction

Eyes, lifted in pleading and in prayer—
Toward what? toward where all prayers ascend:
Heaven's hollow vacancy
And the pure stars' disdain;
O heart, in trembling and in pain
Yearning upward, upward, everywhere—
Unanswered in the end!
If God there be,
Look for Him less in the stars than in the root
Of the elm-tree underfoot
Or grass where the dark cricket sings.
Look down, sometimes, in prayer,
Pray downward toward deep, buried things.
Descend to Him, He may be nearer there.

Anima

". . . The figure of the unknown woman is a personification of the unconscious, which I have called the 'anima' . . . . When projected, the anima always has a feminine form . . ."

                                                              Jung

You came to it through wild country. There the sea's voice
Has sounded always. Rampant meadow and thicket
Bordered it on three sides. The approaches were
By a winding road under tall elms, or circuitous
Woodland paths that led to a slight incline;
From this the house flowed upward as if earth, thrusting
Great trunks of trees up round it, had thrust up
The house itself, in springtime and in summer
Girdled by walls of green. The fresh loam,
Cool from long sleep, flowed up through bole and branches
And out, through branches, into green leaves. Just so
The cool silence of that country flowed
Into green sounds—old oceanic echoes,
Whispers and suspirations of the sea,
Broken at times by surf-bruit, bellowing
Of blind sea-mouths—flowed also into green songs
Hidden among green leaves. The silence there
Had a certain thing to say could not be said
By harp or oboe, flute or violoncello,
Or by the lesser strings; it could not be said
By the human voice; but in sea-sounds you heard it
Perhaps, or in the water-dripping jargon
Of summer birds: endless reiteration
Of chat or vireo, the woodcock's call,

Chirrup and squeegee, larrup, squirt and trill
Of liquid syrinxes—bright drops of song
Spangling the silence. Also, you could compare it,
This silence, to a great rock that the sea's steady
Lament steadily wore away, the acute
Chisel of the thrush's song cut into it,
Cut out small chips of silence, while the clouds,
Those nuns of heaven, paced heaven's corridors,
Robed in Dominican white; the spaces between them,
As they made forward in that grave procession,
Were ceremonial. Or heaven above the green well,
At the bottom of which the house appeared to be lying,
Could be likened, if you preferred, to a huge lens
Focussing the sun's light: the eye of day
Opened and closed again as the cloudy shutter
Shrank or expanded; the shadow patterns sharpened,
Faltered, or stayed, or swayed as the wind's hand
Trembled the leaves. All day long, in the house
Shifting of light and cloud shed light or gloom
Along the passages where the blowing arras
Lifted and settled; the polished surfaces
Of highboy, bureau and hanging mirror darkened
Or brightened as the slant light strengthened or dimmed
From windows opening on the green well of trees;
And into this, at night, the stars looked down,
Or one star, riding in some deep rift of cloud,
Would stare steadily. The wall of green surrounding
The house allowed no view of the outer world,
But in mid-autumn, when the leaves had fallen

And boughs were sere, in the month of wasps, when
        the numbed
Spider starved in his web, when the torpid hornet
Crawled upon casement and curtain, and friendly fires
Kindled on every hearth—suddenly, by chance,
From an upstairs window you might glimpse far off,
Between bare branches, the cold steel-blue of the sea.
And it was early in autumn, he remembered,
Recalling the confused dream (Yet was it a dream?
May it not have been true?), he had returned
To that countryside, on some sad nameless errand
Bent—he would spend the night in the village inn,
So the dream ran—and that evening, while a young moon
Cast her chill fire abroad, he, being seduced
By moonlight and by memory and by longing
To visit the well-loved house, since early boyhood
His summer home, closed for the winter and vacant,
Found himself, from some dark preoccupation
Rousing, and startled to be there, at the very door
Of the old house, and unlocked the door, and entered,
And stood in the moonlit hall. Now, looking back
On that strange evening, it seemed to him its moonlight
Had been no usual moonlight, the shadows it cast,
Like charred substance some cold fire has eaten,
Were blacker, and had something evil about them,
Or so he had felt; yet, mounting the stairs, he found
The long corridor tranced in peaceful light,
And on the garden below him quiet moonlight
Lay like the smile upon a dreaming face,

Cicadas and crickets in the grass made music.
So it had been, he recalled, and how he had stood
At the head of the stairs, listening to what seemed voices
From the farther end of the house, or was it one voice
Calling, for the tone was one? Mere night sounds, perhaps,
And they faded. He moved down the corridor. The rooms
Eastward, and out of reach of the moonlight, glimmered
Vacant and vague as he passed. But now once more,
And nearer, he seemed to hear that voice calling—
Stopped dead, with loud-beating heart. Deep silence followed.
The moonlight dimmed. Excitement seized him. He turned
The corner, and entered the wing of the house, grown dark
Under a clouded moon, and moved toward the bedroom
At the end of the wing, from which the voice had come,
If voice it was, and paused at the threshold, peering
Wide-eyed into the darkness. There he discerned,
But hardly, upon the bed, a figure, supine,
The arms flung upward. He whispered into the darkness,
"Who are you?" and out of the darkness a woman's voice
Sighed, "How long I have waited," and one arm
Descending, with gesture abandoned and absolute
Parted her garments just as the clouded moon
Soared from a cloud to beam on wall and mirror,
And on the bared body, a sudden shaft of light,
Revealing its slenderness, the shadowy places,
The dark fork, pallor of thigh and shoulder—
The face remained obscure. He heard the ocean,
Far-off, call through his dream. Desire, like a flame
Whipped by the wind, leaped up in him. His clothing
Fell from him. Their bodies joined. No word was said.

14

Far off, in dream, he heard the sound of ocean.
Ecstasy mounted. The shaft of moonlight, reaching
Her face, which had lain wholly in shadow, showed him
In an instant of incredulous recognition
His own face, the eyes closed—but oh, how unlike,
Being cast in the mold of woman! And the spasm came,
Making them one. Convulsion took earth and heaven
With a fury of wind, thunder, and a voice that cried
Somewhere out of the chaos, "Spirit has mated
With its own image. No good thing comes of this.
Nothing but dreams." When the fit passed, he was walking
In a meadow shrill with crickets and with starlight,
For the moon had set—and heard, 'Spirit has mated
With its own image. . . . Nothing but dreams.'

Song

Oh, with the hunger of the sea, forever born anew,
  With great waves straining, striving, pouring toward the
    strand,
The sea of my heart's life in exultation moves toward you,
    toward you,
  Unreachable far land!

You are that land; you are the sea of which I am a part
  In love and dream. Like waves beating upon
Trembling shores, the shock and smiting of your loveliness
    upon my heart,
  O dear and lovely one.

The Mask

What is this secret joy
That in all things alive,
Which Time soon shall destroy,
Will flourish still and thrive—
Brute rumor in the blood,
Dim prescience in the heart,
Of some transcendent good
In which they have a part,

Some sense, in each, of all
Bounding its finite will,
Splendor perpetual,
Steadfast, abiding still—
Beyond these accidents
Of change, of death and birth,
The changeless Excellence
That gives all change its worth.

From some deep wisdom springs
The joy all being shares,
The tragedy of things
Is but a mask it wears;
The joy that in the dark
Kindles a million stars
Will hood the ancient spark
In endless woes and wars.

On earth, where joys abound,
Oh, the sheer joy to be!
The heel upon the ground
Goes down in ecstasy,
Or, moved to a brisker measure,
Instep and arch will rise
In dance-rhythm, whose pleasure
Music multiplies.

Such bounty we inherit,
Such dear delight is here,
The heart shall hardly bear it
To know a thing so dear—
In springtime, when the swallow
Veers her windy flight,
When in green dell and hollow
The little leaves hang light.

By meadowland or water,
In ocean, earth, and air,
To swift escape or slaughter
One joy moves everywhere;
For joy the elm-leaf tips
Sway green against the sky,
The fire between joined lips
Is kindled in fierce joy.

For joy, for joy, for joy,
The tragic stage is set;
In tragic masks, for joy
Slayer and slain are met:
Some joy, deep and indwelling,
In all these forms at play,
A joy beyond all telling,
Burns life, burns death away.

Lucifer (a fragment)

Leaving the outposts of last light that shine
Sleepless along infinity's frontier
And the wilderness of matter, he climbed, and came
To the inner citadel, the crowded core,
The swarming glory of heaven, whose bright stream
Round the unwearied truth circles forever . . .

Sunday Morning Moment

The blue flower of day
Widens over these vacant shores
And sea-lands, over the blue vacancy
And bloom of ocean. Now, where the beaches run,
Curving and fading, east and west,
Their tawny road between
The dunes with their tufted green
Pale against a blue sky
And the white line of foam that fringes
The sea-blue sea along a less blue sky,
The mounting sun pours down
His blessing; and on the inland ways,
On Whooping Boys' Hollow and Toilsome Lane
And on the road to Georgica,
His benediction falls. I sit here, musing,
An open book upon my knees.
Great trees bend over me. It is Sunday morning.
From Montauk Highway no murmur. A jet
Gargles its way across heaven, and fades
Seaward. The silence is so great,
Almost I fancy I hear
The wing-beat of the butterfly
Cavorting with happy aimless flight
Over the garden, over the thicket,
In the still light.
I take up my book and read,
At the head of the page,
"O heart, be at peace."

The Passer-by

The rhythm of a piano, and a child's high
Hesitant voice following it; a street,
Empty and dark, that echoes to your feet—
Have you not known it all, O passer-by!

The stars, such aeons away, and from a near
Window soft lamplight pouring, the sudden sense
Of a lost reality's looming imminence,
Sense of the dream in which you are moving here.

Then some dark self within, a secret one,
That always in every thought, in every act,
Upheld you still, will falter, will seem to contract,
Like the pupil of an eye that confronts the sun.

Often, in watchful moments of the night,
Or dreaming, you will have guessed that life is a dream,
Yet these few brief awakenings from it seem
To that dark thing, deep down, too blinding bright.

Drunken Song

In Chingis, where the deep rivers run,
She lifted up the laughing face
No living man has looked upon.
I heard far waters in that place,
The hills stood happy in the sun—
In Chingis, where the deep rivers run,
I laughed into her face.

Dark Joy

1.

What dark Force, striving for more tendrils, more surfaces,
Has multiplied Itself in us as a tree is multiplied in its leaves?
The sleeping One awakens into the many.
We are fragments of a broken Thing,
To be conscious is to be separate.
This is the dark joy of being.
This is the tragedy at the root of being,
For separation brings with it death.
With pain and with death we pay for our separateness.
The Undying is born and dies in Its mortal members.
The great Unity is broken, and self is arrayed against self.
From this all torments flow.
Therefore Jesus preached love, which, in some measure,
    bridges that separation,
And unselfishness, which tempers the fury of the struggle.
Therefore the Buddha preached the need to escape from life
    and death.
Yet all is exchange. Nothing is lost from these siftings.

2.

Exult, and have joy in this day's sun, all living things!
Take delight in his presence today, for it was he who drew
     you forth.
In his presence, you are in the presence of your visible creator.
The Power behind him you are not permitted to behold.
As he is the visible father, the earth is your mother,
And the sea your antecedent mother.
With her, still dwell your elder brothers and sisters,
Who also were fathered of the sun, though they may not
     look upon him.

3.

Exult, all living things, in this life, this moment!

You will not be again, but others shall be, and you will be
those others.

Though life perish from the planet, the planet will give birth
to it once more.

Though the planet be destroyed, new planets shall be created
and will renew it.

Exult, all creatures everywhere, for pain is better than noth-
ingness, and joy is still better.
Exult with the dark joy of being.
Exult, all you whales of the sea!
Exult, all you little foxes that have your dens in the earth!
Exult, you dwellers on distant galaxies!
For to live and to die is good.
So say the crickets and cicadas, all night long, outside my
window here.
So says the oriole who wakes me each morning from the elm
that arches the old house.
So say the ailanthus trees stretching toward it their green
fronds with leaves on either side as many as the feet
of the caterpillar, and every leaf held out to receive the
light.

Mr. X (——State Hospital)

He dreamt he was sleeping, he said, and when he awoke
Found he still was. Then he got all excited,
And had to tell it again—how, for a moment,
He could remember the future, and everything
Turned sad, like music: the timid sound mice
Made on the attic floor, moonlight,
The smile upon her borrowed face.

Helios-Apollo

Noon is heavy
On beach and dune
Of this blazing coast
In mid-July's
Radiance, the massive
Waters move
Ponderously here
Their lagging weight—
The weight of waters
Burdens the planet.
Great breakers, thundering,
Drag, as they fall,
Other breakers with them,
And pull the pale flounce
Of foam along the shore,
To gulp and chuckle,
Gurgle and wash,
Of tumbling waters.

Pure vacancy
Of sand, sea, sky
To the clear horizon,
Heaven without cloud
Except for those
High traceries, flourishes,
Left where the wind's
Invisible hand
Has scribbled his signature—

Abstract design
Arching the ocean.

Here, by the old
Pavilion with its weathered
Shingles, the beach
Is thronged with bathers,
Watchers, idlers
Under gay umbrellas,
The fat man, the proud
Mother—her darling
Surveys, unabashed,
The infinite ocean,
Also radios,
Picknickers, sun-glasses,
Water-wings, beach hats,
Gulls—here a sage
Meditates seaward,
And there a young girl,
With shapely torso
And trunks that barely
Cover where the slender
Legs divide from,
Lies supine
To the raging light,
As Danäe once
To the golden shower.

Oh, deadlier than
Coiled cobra the arch
Of thigh and bosom
So snugly banded;
Stronger, more cruel
Than his venom, the curves
Of that innocent body!

But, look, in the water
The bathers, plunging
Through the combers, riding
Their surf-boards, the timid
Dabbling at the sea's
Edges—happy
Shouting and laughter
Of boys and girls,
And children screaming
In the surging spume.

Ah, not as once,
With flutes and lyres
Or ritual dance,
Are you praised and adored,
Ineffable father,
Helios-Apollo—
The clouds are dispersed
Revealing a god,
Where you stand at the center,
The navel of heaven.

Glad giver of joy,
May the happy cries,
The delight and the laughter,
Of these your children,
Spawn of your fire
On golden shores,
Be our hymn to you, father,
Life-giver, light-bringer,
Maker of all,
Noticed of none—
Though truly the sun-bathers
Worship you well,
Hushed here before you.

O father, I, too,
Caressed by a star!
Your light reaches me
Across the abysses
Where your step is thunder,
Your cyclonic fury.
Yet touch me tenderly
Now, where I lie,
Open as a flower
To the mercy of your glance;
Let your hand be ever
Gentle upon us,
Who are your creatures,
Fire of your fire;

Father, creator,
Whom none has dared look upon,
Terrible beauty,
Of which the bright moon
Is but as a mirror,
A pale reflection—
Oh, of what are you mirror
And pale reflection,
Intolerable glory,
Godhead of light?

Return in Age

Dark sound of the sea, soft shadow of the sea
Between blurred dunes that cup this quiet place,
Vast shores, vague night—how sharply memory
Brings it all back, your step, your voice, your face,
On nights long lost that brought you here to me,
With a low sound, with a soft low sound of the sea:

The fear of your coming, terror lest you should not come,
Oh, insupportable waiting, the insane
Anguish and joy, longing's delirium—
The kiss first given and taken and given again,
The words said over and over endlessly,
To a low sound, to a soft low sound of the sea.

Vast odor of the sea, soft shuffle of the sea
Along waste shores—what memory shall assuage
The heart burdened with many a memory!
The youth that was now stands here in old age,
A stranger to himself. O love no more to be,
First love, young love, wild love, come back to me,
With a low sound, with a soft low sound of the sea!

Reverie on the Nature of Things

Divine glory of things,
Dread pain, implacable hunger, it is enough!
Heaven and earth are full of you: wide wings
Over the water, where the fish-hawk hangs alert;
Over the field, where the falcon spies the dove;
At the wood's edge, the doe,
Torn by the wolves, from many a crimson hurt
Rilling her blood into the snow;
And, in the ocean's dark,
Fear gliding, horror gliding, masks of doom,
Lit by some inner spark,
Groping their way along the gloom;
Each from the other divided by the one need,
To maintain selfhood, to destroy
Life in the name of life; all by one joy
United, lust to perpetuate the breed;
On earth, in sea, in heaven,
By fierce necessity driven.

The fledgling eaglet at daybreak takes the untried
Air road over the mountain pass, and soars
The valley for his prey;
The young lion in his pride,
At dusk of day,
Crouching, with ruffled mane,
Out of the shadow of the jungle roars
Into the jungle night
Hunger's challenge and proclamation:

Everywhere, since time began,
Terror and exultation,
Strange beauty, cruel delight,
Murder that refreshes and restores,
Death and pain—
Brute against brute, man against man,
In endless wars.

It is enough! Oh, for some Orphean finger
To touch the sacred string,
Whose pure vibrations while they linger
Shall force the forbidden secret and unloose
Such music as will bring
The great remission, the desired truce
To the long warfare, the old suffering.
At that new sound, first heard,
Then should all creatures gather,
Man, beast, and bird,
And know themselves the same,
All creation come together;
Opponents in the blind strife
And bloody war of life
Consort as comrades without fear or blame;
And, the mask fallen from the enemy,
Our brother, our true love, we there should see,
Fated antagonist in the mystery,
A fellow creature, sharing our sufferings,
Sharing our doom—victim, as we,
Of the harsh law of things.

Oh, that it might be done:
All wars and struggles cease,
Mankind have peace,
All creatures know themselves at last as one.

Marvellous beauty of things,
Incomprehensible beauty, it is enough!
The delicate patterns in the pollened stuff
That is like powder upon the wood-nymph's wings;
The wide flower of the sea,
Folding and unfolding endlessly
Its fringes of pale foam;
The ardor that shines through
Where the great clouds at close of day draw home
To their burial in the west—
Headlands of fire, washed by cerulean blue,
Seraphic shores of light,
The islands of the blest,
Resolute against the encroaching night;
Dread beauty, the boar's tusks, the tiger's fangs;
The intricate web, tenuous as a sigh,
In which the spider hangs,
Where innocent, air-borne things shall die;
The python's mottled and muscled length,
Thicker than a man's thigh,
His sleeping strength;
Tragic beauty of all things alive,
To these perpetual wars
Condemned, to perish or survive,

37

Each with the other to strive,
In the iron arena of the indifferent stars.

Here, too, under the sign of pain and death,
Love draws its breath
And plays its tender part
To the one end:
The love of friend for friend;
Pity of the compassionate heart—
The mother's downward glance
And smiling countenance;
The love of man and woman,
Oh, fiery torment, all devouring flame,
Transport half godlike, half sub-human,
Rapture between
The sacred and the obscene,
Grotesque union, in which desire and shame
Kindle each other, how may we celebrate
The way by which we came,
The narrow gate
That is the gate to embodiment through birth,
The lowly door
By which the spirit comes to earth.

It is enough! The heart will hold no more.
After the three-score years and ten,
Participant and spectator too
Of the great drama, what is there left to do,
All being done and said,
But praise and praise, again and yet again,

But worship and adore,
The beautiful, mischievous, dread,
Sublime, implacable Spirit at the core
Of all things made.

Evening deepens, the solemn splendor of light
Deepens to a subdued
Radiance over meadow and wood
In this green solitude,
And the approaching night
Brings with it an exalted mood:
All I have loved seem suddenly very near,
The dusk is thronged
With presences out of old days and places,
Those I have cherished, and some that I have wronged—
The well remembered faces,
The living and the dead, they all are here.
"Forgive me," I cry,
"All that was done out of necessity;
We are woven on the one loom,
All we are tangled together in the one doom;
My brother, my own blood, forgive me," I cry—
"And you, dumb sacrificial creatures
Whose lives have fed our own,
Body and bone,
You without name or features,
Forgive us," I cry,
"The murders we have done
Under the sun,
Out of that same necessity."

Oh, may all we that are one,
So horribly at war with each other, so driven
By the one plight—oh, may we learn to forgive
And be forgiven; for all that live,
Because of that have need to be forgiven.

Soon the high stars come on.
The night is full of voices and of dreams—
Memories of those long gone,
Of those still here,
Equally dear.
All that is vanished seems
Transfigured now. Cast up by the blind storm
Of being, little timid fluttering things
Out of the darkness swarm
In longing wild and vain,
Beating against the window-pane
Their tender wings.

Evening-Star

Now, at dusk, while grasshoppers are shrilling
Endlessly their song into my ears,
You, great star, have come in silence, stilling
Me with light across ten million years.

What is song! Your silences are thunder
To a spirit listening silently—
You, such light years off, and I, oh wonder,
I a part of you, as you of me.

You in the slow fire of time are turning,
Time, whose fury tortures flesh and stone;
I, like you, in that still flame am burning,
Living, giving, dying, and alone.

Interlude

The March of Science

"American scientists working with cats have encountered evidence that certain areas of the brain are responsible for the elusive condition called 'paying attention'." The New York *Times*, May 12, 1959.

American scientists working with cats
(Such work, surely, merits some mention)
Have encountered definitive evidence
That certain areas of the brain
(And this seems to make sense)
Are responsible for the elusive condition called 'paying attention'.

So when Sappho (if that is the name of your cat),
Eluding all solicitation,
Sits arching her neck and sleeking the fur
In the crook of her neck, that's so hard to get at,
Don't argue with her—
Look up where those areas lie in the brain, and apply stimulation.

In dealing with cats, even more than with men
(The findings here are conclusive),
Discussion is vain: get to work on the brain,
Treat those areas rough till you spark some response—
Or learn, to your pain,
That a cat can be calm, at times almost too calm, and extremely elusive.

Earth

(with apologies to *The New Yorker*)

"A planet doesn't explode of itself," said drily
The Martian astronomer, gazing off into the air—
"That they were able to do it is proof that highly
Intelligent beings must have been living there."

Dialogue After Bishop Berkeley

"You mean to say," I said,
"I made up the universe out of my head?"

"Sure," he said.

"I'm amazed," I said.

"Go on! You know it's so.
I know you know."

"What you mean?" I said.

"I mean like I said.
You made up the universe out of your head,
And maintain it still
By an act of will."

"You sure that's true?"

"Sure. All that worrying you do
Keeps the grass green and the sky blue."

"Gosh," I said,
"What'll happen when I die?"

"You won't have time to know I was right—
The whole damn thing'll go out like a light."

"You mean that?" I said.

"Sure," he said.
"Why don't you try?
It's nice to try."

Night-Piece

There were footsteps on the stairway, uncertain
Sounds he had never heard, more like the flopping
Of a chicken than the tread of a man. The night
Tensed, and he waited. Yet soon
All was quiet, and he could relax—first, though,
Take a look-see. Nothing there. Then,
Perplexed but in bed once more,
Suddenly, in that moment when he was about
To fall asleep, he
Fell asleep.

Hippopotamothalamium

A hippopotamus had a bride
   Of rather singular beauty,
When he lay down at her side
   'Twas out of love, not duty—
   Hers was an exceptional beauty.
Take, oh take those lips away, etc.

He met her in Central Nigeria,
   While she was resident there,
Where life is distinctly superior
   And a hippo can take down her hair—
   And, God, but she was fair!
Take, oh take those lips away, etc.

She was coming up from her morning swim
   When first they chanced to meet:
He looked at her, she looked at him,
   And stood with reluctant feet
   Where mud and river meet.
Take, oh take those lips away, etc.

Their eye-beams, twisted on one thread,
   Instantaneously did twine,
And he made up poetry out of his head,
   Such as: "Dear heart, be mine"—
   And he quoted, line for line,
"Hail to thee, blithe spirit", etc.

Now, hippopotamoid courtesy
  Is strangely meticulous—
A beautiful thing, you will agree,
  In a hippopotamus—
  And she answered, briefly, thus:
"*Hail to thee, blithe spirit*", etc.

Perhaps she was practising the arts
  That grace old Hippo's daughter,
The coquetries that win all hearts,
  For, even as he besought her,
  She slid into the water.
Out, out, brief candle, etc.

Now, on the borders of the wood,
  Whence love had drawn him hither,
He paces in an anguished mood,
  Darting hither and thither
  In a terrific dither.
Out, out, brief candle, etc.

The course of true love never yet
  Ran smooth, so we are told,
With thorns its pathway is beset
  And perils manifold,
  So was it from of old.
Out, out, brief candle, etc.

Yet soon a happier morning smiles,
    The marriage feast is spread—
The flower girls were crocodiles,
    When hippopotamus led
    Hippopotamus, with firm tread,
    A bride to the bridal bed.
Milton, thou should'st be living at this hour.

Colloquy

"It isn't fair. It isn't fair.
What's the good of being dead
If you won't know that you are?" he said.

"You silly ass, to give a care!
You won't be there, you'll be everywhere,
And somebody else'll be there instead."

FOUR STUDIES IN THE BIG I

1. *The Big I*

A bird with a big eye
In at my open window poked his head,
And fixed me with a big eye.
"Who are you? What do you want?" I said.
"Me? You mean you don't know me?" he made reply,
"Why, I am I. Who are you?"
"I, too, am I," I bashfully admitted.
Now here was a big I-dea to work upon,
For if each one is I, must we not all be one?
Then I am one in all, and all are one in me.
I observed, thinking it over carefully,
That I wondered, this being true,
What made us feel so separate, so alone.
"*I did,*" shouted the bird,
And I turned to strangle him, but he was flown.

2. Child and Universe

"How shall I tell the child about God?"
This was the question Timmy's mother put
To her father, the Reverend Brown,
Whose wisdom in matters theological
She regarded as absolute.
He, taking his spectacles off
And putting on his frown,
Suggested, after a slightly affected cough,
"This summer, when you and Timmy are out of town
On some beautiful cloudless night,
Take the boy out under the vast expanse
Of the starry summer sky,
And ask him, 'Who made all this?'
The child will be at a loss to reply.
Then is your chance."
And the mother did
As she was bid—
And on a cloudless windless night in July
When the hollow of heaven, like an inverted cup,
Was bright with stars to the very brim,
And the universe hung glittering over him,
She lifted the child up,
And pointed to it, and said,
"Timmy, who made all this?" And the unabashed boy
Without a moment's hesitation answered, "Tim."

3. You Bet

Well, you know Jed, how he can talk kinda' tough—
Like, you know,
Dirty words, an' all—
So, one day, he says something real mean to Joe,
And Joe, he figgers he had about enough
From this bozo, and he talks right back, and Jed
Steps up to'm, and he says, "Which way you wanna fall?"
Now, you know Joe wouldn't stand for no such guff,
Not from no one, not from you nor me,
No, Siree—
He's a'goin' to teach that guy to throw his weight around;
And, by golly, if he doesn't sail right into Jed!
You bet, hot damn!
And Jed felled him to the ground.

4. Purely Personal

Dr. Smith, professor and lecturer extraordinary
Before women's clubs, on poetics and "creative writing",
Samples of which said ladies would submit to him,
With results not always too exciting,
In his closing lecture, after having thanked them all,
Ventured he had only one criticism to make,
To wit: that women in general
Took everything, perhaps, a bit too personally—
"There are some of you," he said, "will take
In a purely personal way
Whatever I may say."
Whereupon Miss Minnie Dumont,
Rising to get the professor's attention,
In a proud clear voice, as was her wont,
Gave the lie to the dazed professor's contention,
With,
"Please, Dr. Smith,
I don't."

The Grand Hierarchy

In nature's order, the grand hierarchy
Of snakes and poets, bankers, swallows, skunks,
There is an underlying unity
Embracing all, whatever they may be:
Bishops or archbishops,
Angels or archangels,
Monks or chipmunks.

Part Two

Song on Reaching Seventy

Shall not a man sing as the night comes on?
He would be braver than the bird
That shrieks for terror, and is gone
Into the gathering dark; and he has heard
Often, at evening's hush,
Upon some towering sunset bough
A belated thrush
Lift up his heart against the menacing night,
Till silence covered all. Oh, now
Before the coming of a greater night,
How bitterly sweet and dear
All things have grown! How shall we bear the brunt,
The fury and joy of every sound and sight,
Now almost cruelly fierce with all delight:
The clouds of dawn that blunt
The spearhead of the sun; the clouds that stand,
Raging with light, around his burial;
The rain-pocked pool
At the wood's edge; a bat's skittering flight
Over the sunset-colored land;
Or, heard toward morning, the cock pheasant's call!
Oh, every sight and sound
Has meaning now! Now, also, love has laid
Upon us her old chains of tenderness,
So that to think of the belovèd one,
Love is so great, is to be half afraid—
It is like looking at the sun,
That blinds the eye with truth.

Yet longing remains unstilled,
Age will look into the face of youth
With longing, over a gulf not to be crossed.
Oh, joy that is almost pain, pain that is joy,
Unimaginable to the younger man or boy—
Nothing is quite fulfilled,
Nothing is lost;
But all is multiplied, till the heart almost
Aches with its burden: there and here
Become as one, the present and the past;
The dead, who were content to lie
Far from us, have consented to draw near—
We are thronged with memories,
Move amid two societies,
And learn at last
The dead are the only ones who never die.

Great night, hold back
A little longer yet your mountainous, black
Waters of darkness from this shore,
This island garden, this paradisal spot,
The haunt of love and pain,
Which we must leave, whether we would or not,
And where we shall not come again.
More time—oh, but a little more,
Till, stretched to the limits of being, the taut heart break,
Bursting the bonds of breath,
Shattering the wall
Between us and our world, and we awake
Out of the dream of self into the truth of all,
The price for which is death.

The Sun Men Call It

Stars have their glory and, or near or far,
Are worth our worship, as all glories are;
There is a star I worship, early and late—
The sun men call it, drinking from that great
Fountain of light, the glory of a star.

The Divine Insect

Already it's late summer. Sun-bathers go
Earlier now. Except for those who lie
Dazed between sea-music and radio
The beach is bare as the blue bowl of the sky,
Where a cloud floats, solitary and slow.

And up the beach, where at mid-summer's height
One gull with occasional lurch and pause would steer
Onward his leisurely loose-winged casual flight,
Gull wings weave patterns, their noise floods the ear
Like a fugue, cry answering cry in hoarse delight.

Now on the beach there also may be found,
Straddled in mimic flight, with arching wing
Spread either way, some gull swift death has downed
There, like a tumbled kite whose severed string
Kept it in heaven by binding it to the ground.

Inland, when the slant evening sun-beams touch
Leaves, long obscured in tunnelled shade, to flame,
The divine insect, for I called him such,
Begins his high thin music. To my shame
I never learned what he was, who owe him so much.

Listening to his frail song, so pure, so dim,
I made my poems, he was mystery's decoy,
Something far and lost, just over the rim
Of being, or so I felt, and as a boy
I wove fantastic notions about him.

Throughout long evenings and hushed midnights when
Grasshoppers shrilled, his barely perceptible note
Wound on like a thread of time, while my pen
Made its own scratchy music as I wrote.
The divine insect and I were comrades then.

That high hypnotic note opened some door
On a world seemingly come upon by chance,
But a world, surely, I had known before.
Deeper I sank into a timeless trance—
Strange thoughts and fancies troubled me more and more.

I could pass through that minuscule sound, it seemed to me,
As through a fine tube, getting smaller and still more small,
Until I was smaller than nothing—then, suddenly,
Come to the other end of the tube, and crawl
Out, into glittering immensity.

For, if by travelling west you shall come east
Or, as Einstein has it, the continuum
Curves on itself, may we not through the least
Come to the largest, and so finally come
Back where we were, undiminished and unincreased?

Since then, I have tried to put this into verse,
But language limits the sense it often mars—
I still believe, for better or for worse,
We look through one atom into all the stars,
In the note of one insect hear the universe.

These few green acres where so many a day
Has found me, acres I have loved so long,
Have the whole galaxy for crown, and stay
Unspoiled by that. Here in some thrush's song
I have heard things that took my breath away.

It is a country out of the world's ken,
Time has no power upon it. Year on year,
Summer unfolds her pageant here again—
I have looked deep into all being here
Through one loved place far from the storms of men.

Here often, day and night, there will be heard
The sea's grave rhythm, a dark undertone
Beneath the song of insect or of bird—
Sea-voices by sea-breezes landward blown,
And shudder of leaves by the soft sea-wind stirred.

In the jade light and gloom of woodland walks
The spider lily and slender shinleaf stand,
The catbird from his treetop pulpit talks
The morning up, and in the meadowland
The velvet mullein lift their woolly stalks.

The world grows old. Ageless and undefiled
These stay, meadow and thicket, wood and hill:
The green fly wears her golden dress, the wild
Grape is in bloom, the fork-tailed swallow still
Veers on the wind as when I was a child.

And in mid-August, when the sun has set
And the first star out of the west shows through,
The divine insect, as I call him yet,
Begins his high thin note, so pure, so true,
Putting me ever deeper in his debt.

The old enchantment takes me as before,
I listen, half in dream, hearing by chance
The soft lapse of the sea along the shore,
And sink again into that timeless trance,
Deeper and deeper now, and more and more.

A Memory Out of Childhood

Stiff in their Sunday best, the two brothers,
Wide-eyed and motionless, would hang upon
The sound of that familiar voice, the mother's.

Her quiet voice as it read on and on
Held them intent through endless fairy-tales,
Jumble of witches foiled and maidens won,

Enchanted woods with talking nightingales,
And frogs proved to be princes in disguise—
Absurdities whose sorcery never fails.

And when her hand, before their very eyes,
As if by magic that it could command,
Turning the page in which the dragon dies,

Opened fresh vistas into fairyland
And a lost world that was too sweet to last,
Their gaze would rest a moment on that hand—

Dear hand, itself long since one with the past.

House in Bonac

The old house lay there like a great ship foundered
At the bottom of green sea-water. From its windows
Westward or eastward, south or north, you saw,
As at the bottom of shallow water, green
Of encroaching thicket and wood—wild green
Of oak and elm, sycamore, cherry, ailanthus,
Threatening garden and house. Through crowding leaves
Green light filtered down like silt, wavering
And weak as light in shaded water, and rested
In patterns on the grassy floor. The frame of the house
Was sagging and crumbling, ivy and honeysuckle
Had thrust great webs of green across the windows
And over porch railings—and he had returned
After long absence. It was June, and wet
With chill sea-fog and dew, branches dripping
Their dew on last year's leaves made pattering sounds,
And somewhere, as always, a thrush was singing. He stood
And listened to it. Here, looking south and west
Into a garden now greenly overgrown,
Was the room with his father's desk and the music rack
That held the score for his father's French horn—how often
Those rounded tones, Brahms perhaps or Schubert,
Tones so full and round you could almost touch them,
Had floated dreamily from this room. Next to it,
A larger room, looking south and east, was his mother's—
So strangely diminished, so far away she seemed,
He thought, caressing with his eyes her brightly
Embroidered runners over bureau and table,

Her hand-bound books on the shelves. Opening on this,
Was the nursery, facing east, so that sometimes dawn,
Slanting its level light on wall and ceiling,
Would wake his brother and himself, they lolled
In their four-posters, finding in knot and blemish
Of the dark cedar-wood rafters overhead
Figures and faces around which they wove stories,
Till Fräulein Maison came and ordered them up.
Now all were gone, of that small flock none
Remained but himself, and the great hall downstairs,
With its wide fireplace and its oil lamp hung
From a girder over the table where they gathered
To talk or read aloud through warm evenings
While the cricket plucked his harp and the shrill, prolonged
Stridulation of grasshoppers flooded the summer night,
Was silent as a barn loft when swallows go,
Was vacant as a dark house full only of moonlight.
Two thrushes were singing now; they seemed to be
Answering each other. A flicker rapped out his tattoo.
It was mid-day, the sea-fog lightened. And now he came
To the room that had been his as a boy and, later,
As a young man: two windows facing east,
Between them a table and chair; along the north wall
A fireplace and a bureau, above it a mirror
And, farther on, a shelf crowded with books;
By the south wall a highboy and, beside it,
But nearer the windows, a bed. Familiar room,
Where youth's old drama was enacted anew,
Room where first love first laid its bitter-sweet
Spell on a dreaming boy, where clear voices

From over the rim of the world, the rim of time,
Swinburne and Heine, Dante, Baudelaire, Keats,
Shook a boy's heart, and always through them all,
Mysterious as the rhythm of his own blood,
Felt rather than heard, the one voice,
The sea's voice, her shudder along far shores,
Widening the kingdoms of imagination,
Till love and the sea and poetry were one
In a joy almost too much to bear. Torments
Of youth—torment of bodily longing, torment
Of the spirit's hunger, and these often at war,
One with the other: what agonies, what doubts,
What illusory triumphs this small room had known
On nights when the will-o'-the-wisp of poetry,
That wilful demon, that phantom, that chimera,
Tortured him into sleeplessness—he lay
As in trance, compelled by the metronome of the cricket,
Hearing within that sound another sound,
Another meaning behind its immediate meaning,
His listening spirit stretched wide apart, until,
The poem, achieved—or so he would think—morning,
Sending its first light through the windows, found him,
His fallen, defeated head sunk deep in dreams
Where one face still, truer than any poem
He ever could make, and more full of mockery
Than all the poems of the masters he so envied,
Looked out, with laughing lips and slanted eyes
Over high cheekbones—a face shy as a gypsy's,
Too innocent to be kind, that had thrust its thorn
Into his very blood. Intolerable longing,

71

Intolerable hope, intolerable joy, moments
When for sheer ecstasy he fell to his knees,
In adoration, he did not know of what,
In gratitude, to whom he could not say,
For all was one, and nameless; Time had not yet
Set limits to imagination's kingdoms
Or dwindled the boundaries of the possible world.
Standing there in the doorway, he looked about him.
The room was still unchanged. And what was it he heard
Far off, a sound older than memory?
Murmur of oceanic waters, echoes,
Familiar to these shores. Nothing was changed.
The old books leaned along the shelf, the old
Blotter and pen were on the table as always,
But the strange being who had inhabited here,
Roaming these fields by moonlight, pacing these beaches,
Walking these woods in a fever of to and fro,
Lying awake all night to listen to a cricket,
Trying to translate the way its music was—
That innocent, ardent, foolish, hopeful creature,
His earlier self, whom he no longer knew,
Had perished, and he could look upon him now
As a stranger, from a great distance, with compassion,
With tenderness, as from a father to a son.
Thrushes were singing again, and their voices
Blended with the sea's voice, and he recalled
How these had never, for him, been voices merely
But, through them, angelic voices had seemed to speak
Into his heart, with deliberate intent,
Of marvellous things, present and yet to come,

Widening the kingdoms of imagination.
And the voices were still unchanged. Or were they un-
        changed?
Surely, they were unchanged? He paused to listen.
Did the far sea now have a different sound,
The thrush's song lack something? Slowly he knew:
It was himself that was changed, he had grown old
Living too long in dreams, and all these voices,
Through which the angelic voices had seemed to speak,
So full once of divine, strange future things,
Were now merely voices out of the past,
His past, for he was a portion of that past.
It was the past cried out to him from this place
Whose venom so early was planted in his veins,
So bitterly loved, so bitterly hated too;
How often, half in loathing, half in longing,
How many a year, he had returned to it,
Self-driven, against his will, and felt the magic
That was mortal there—dark music of thrushes,
The sea's monotony, an evening-star
Hung light-years deep down vistas of trembling shade,
Dear rooms and corridors where the belovèd dead
Live on, long after, like voices in memory,
And murmur of insects, timeless, without end—
Cast its old spell upon him, drawing him back
Into the kingdoms of imagination,
Which now had become the kingdoms of the past,
So that, summer on summer, year on year,
Sinking bemused, enchanted, unaware,
Deeper and deeper into the web of dream,

The past had overtaken him, he had been taken
Prisoner by that past. He stood still and pondered,
Trying to understand. He thought, if the future
Becomes the present, the present becomes the past,
In the great flux and mystery of things,
May it not be, since all is circular
And the infinite stream of the stars rounds on itself—
May it not be, he thought, puzzling, that somehow
You might contrive to reach through the past to a future
That would be the past coming back to you again
Or, rather, your coming back again to it,
For it is you who move? What, he wondered,
If in this house of childhood, with its rooms
Where those, beloved and cherished in some past
That now was but a legend, still lived on
Like names in a legend—what, if in this old house,
Haunt of the past, he should abandon himself
Utterly to that past, go down, give over,
Sink back into that past, and let the enchantment
Work out its will, till gradually he felt,
As the courtiers in the fairy tale, dark sleep
Thrust its soft bondage upon limbs and senses—
A strange, a wizard, a compulsive sleep,
Like the web the spider spins, like the cocoon
Woven by the larva against some great awakening—
Wrap round him its slow drowsiness, and draw him
Downward into its darkness, as he lay,
Spellbound, upon his bed, in deepening trance,
Infinite languor, lassitude supreme,
Bottomless night? Season on changing season,

74

Year upon year would visit him; winds of autumn,
Crying in the broken eaves, shake the old house;
Rain and snow seep through the rotting shingles;
The rafters crumble, girder and beam go down
In rubble and dust; wild voices of spring,
The phoebe's plaint, the oriole's cheerful carol,
Call to him where he lay; and he sleep on,
Through summer's long decline, the murmur of insects,
The cricket's tune, the far sound of the sea—
Unmindful if the sun from the rim of morning
Cast its cold light on wall and mirror; careless
If moon or star peered through the rifted ceiling
At nightfall, or of the little moths that came
Brushing his face with their soft wings; unheeding
If dusk or dawn, winter or summer. Mice
Would gnaw at the fallen timbers, and the spider
Hang her grey veil between them, while from porch
Or void casement, at twilight, the whip-poor-will
Shouted his lament above the tangled ruins
With honeysuckle part overgrown, mouldering
Back into earth, half-married to earth already;
And he sleep on, unmoved, untouched, secure,
Full of black night, sinking deeper and deeper
Into the kingdoms of imagination,
Whose limits border upon the kingdom of death.
Why, then, he thought, standing by the stair and musing
On these strange fancies, this still stranger sleep,
Might there not be, if he could abandon himself
Utterly to that sleep, its sheer abysses,
Give up, go down, descend, aeon beyond aeon,

Dark beyond dark, depth beyond depth, to the very
Pit, the impenetrable core where the night is rooted—
Might there not be, Time's wheel having come full circle,
Some great awakening, the past become the future,
And all be before him again, as once at birth?
All the joy and the pain of things: the meadowlark's piercing
Note in meadows of childhood on that first day
Of return to the country home, odors of ocean,
Odors of cedarwood rafters and logs burning
On the broad hearth, and the sound of his father's French
        horn
From the little upstairs room, and his mother's gentle
Irish voice reading aloud to them
From *The Golden Treasury* or some story book,
On rainy mornings in the first green of May—
All should come back, the joy and the pain of things,
The hour of hope fulfilled and the hour of heartbreak,
And youth, and all that longing, his dear true love's
Shy gypsy face under the flowerlike hair,
The look so brave, so serious—all should come back,
All should be found again, in that fury of life,
The passion of it, the wonder and the glory,
In voices of wind and water, bird and poet,
The sea's voice and the voice of his own blood;
And always, through them all, those other voices,
The angelic voices, speaking into his heart,
Of marvellous things, present and yet to come,
Widening the kingdoms of imagination
To the limitless dream of youth. He turned, and listened—
For what, he hardly knew. No thrushes were singing.
Far off he heard the sound of the sea.

Hour Before Sleep

Evening—and I, in the hour before sleep,
Lean out once more, and stare
Skyward, at you, bright star, deep, deep
Down some black well of darkness sunken there,
Some bottomless pit in heaven's towering steep:
Sorrowful revelation, secret laid bare
In the dark hour before sleep,
Secret too dark to share—
Forgotten, with the approach of sleep.

Dialectics of Flight

To get off the ground has always been difficult
For poet or bird, and the gray gull
At the sea's edge here, who regards me with an eye
That is sceptical, shall we say, would never try
To scale heaven by direct assault—
Ascent is always oblique and casual.

But the wings must be kept ready. He stretches his wings
To keep them ready; those huge vans,
Feathered, curving forefingers, reach upward again,
Arch outward, are shaken, are slowly lowered; and then,
With curious rufflings and fidgetings,
Fold back onto the body like collapsed fans.

The sea's blue crescent, the harsh smell of the sea,
Her thunders, this perpetual roar,
These vacant beaches, are background for a bird
With whom I have always wanted to have a word—
Theories of flight interest me.
I advance upon him boldly along the shore

And begin: "O master of ascent"—
When, suddenly, the great wings on either side
Canopy out; with lumbering gait he runs
Into the wind; then, all at once
(So imperceptible was the event),
Is mounted upon the wind his wings bestride.

He climbs seaward, leaving me breathless here.
Now, as he travels, gaining height,
Those two webbed feet, symbolic of his birth,
His bondage to sea and earth,
Are quietly retracted, landing gear
Needed for the interval between flight and flight.

This Our Life

The work of wind and wave is never done,
The stars keep timeless vigil; this, our life,
Is to their high, austere fidelity
As is the idle jigging of a fife
To the great task and silence of the sun,
The termless roar and labor of the sea.

Morning After Rain

For days it had "literally",
As my grandmother put it, "rained cats and dogs."
Toward dawn it cleared, the unblemished sky
Shone soft pewter. I got up early this morning
And walked under the elms and down
The glade, with an eye on the weather,
Hoping that it would hold. Already,
Small lapdog clouds with a curious fixed
Air of determination were moving
Forward, onward, eastward, forward,
Across heaven, to heaven knows where.
Earth smelled of rain and dew, the foliage
Sparkled in the fresh jungle of green
On either side, where birds flashed in and out,
Shaking down raindrops, eyes of water
The sun looked into, that glittered up into mine
Out of the grass. Suddenly they came over,
The wild swans, in close formation—
Three of them. I have always held
That the bird who glides on motionless wing
Gets transportation for very little, but these
Great hulks oared their laborious way,
With stretched-out necks and synchronous rhythm,
Solemnly, slowly, pontifically,
Over my head, the huge wings
Going whoosh, whoosh, as they departed
Westward. Where the day-lily stood
In her pride of being, I bent over

To touch a slender blossom opening
Toward the first sunlight, and forgot
The wild swans. But all morning
I was haunted, not by them
So much as by the thought of the air
That had carried those bulky forms, its firmness,
What it is like to be a bird
And feel under your wings, as a swimmer
The water under his arms, the resilience
You push against bearing you up,
Its flow and ripple along the feathers—
To launch upon it and know in joy
The solidity on which you learn to rest
Your confident weight and body, who are
A swimmer in the air. And other
Thoughts about the air were with me
All day: how every word we speak
Is made of a mouthful of it, the poem,
The real one, the one spoken,
Made of the air such billions of us,
Over the centuries, have breathed
And then let go, so that, as Rilke said,
We have been father to many a tempest,
As the dead before us were, whose life-breath
We breathe again into new words,
New prayers, new poems, and which, again surrendered,
Those after us shall use, in their turn,
For it is inexhaustible; also, how
This air, without smell, without taste,
Colorless, wholly invisible,

Will float, nevertheless, the burdened
Tonnage of air-liners with all their freight,
As though they were downy feathers, or topple
A town, in its fury, and provoke
Waves till they whiten with anger; it is
The protective ocean on whose floor
We move about, and without whose protection
The sun's rage, or the absolute
Zero, on his departure, would shrivel us
To cinders. But chiefly I thought of it
As the fostering breast from which we suck
The milk of life; laughing or sobbing,
Talking, working, even asleep,
With every breath we draw it in,
That heavenly food on which, from the first
Cry to the final gasp groping for it,
We have depended all our days.
Oh, how reluctantly in the end
We are weaned from that bountiful and kindly
Breast, whose unfailing sustenance,
More necessary than bread or water,
We cannot lack for long! Tomorrow,
In the early morning, when breathing is sweetest,
I plan, should the weather hold, to walk
Under the elms once more and down
The path in the woods still wet with rain,
Shining with dew and happy birdsong—
Song made of crystal morning air,
Dripping of water on cool leaves—
And have, perhaps, if only a glimpse

Of the striped chipmunk as he hurries
Across the open, for a dread
Moment, between cover and cover
Of dark undergrowth and shady grass.

Testament

You still forms and modes of the creation,
Charged with meaning for my spirit here
In its torment, in its exultation,
To your voices let me be an ear.

Cloud and mountain, rock and tree and flower,
Let me win you into me, to dwell
Deeply there till, wholly in my power,
You have told me what you have to tell.

Let my spirit, howsoever fleeting,
Be a meeting-place for root and star,
Where all meanings gather and, in meeting,
Learn from one another what they are.

O great Life, as I grow wiser, older,
Let me not, grown timid, close the door
On your tragic truth but, humbler, bolder,
Force it open wider more and more.

Orbit of some star through heaven sweeping,
Through my spirit let that orbit be—
Lashes on a girl's cheek wet from weeping,
When they're lifted curve their arc through me.

The Face

He was aware, in his dream, of a face bending over his—
a face, neither man's nor woman's, of such transcendent
beauty, force, laughing tenderness, and delight, as marked
it not of this earth. A pang, some premonition of death itself,
struck through him, and he struggled, but his struggles served
only to increase the sense of gradual absorption into another
being and of the dissolution of his own. The very core of his
selfhood seemed about to be dissolved away, and he started
up in frenzy, when that face of inexorable compassion trans-
fixed him with a smile, a glance, so divine, that in an instant
all was comprehended. He yielded; his heart overflowed, pouring on to meet this exultant love. And, in that instant, as he
surrendered what so desperately, since the hour of birth, he
had fought to preserve, it became clear to him that this was
the goal toward which, without knowing it, he had, his whole
life long, been laboring with every breath he drew. Time fell
away. All consciousness of self was lost. There remained only
the face and his adoration of it. Then this, too, passed. He
had become part of what he loved.

The Timid Future

Wind in the eaves of the old house, wind over Russia
And the English coast, wind over the forelands
Of Europe, over the beaches of Long Island,
Autumnal wind, wailing the world sorrow,
With demon voices thronged, lewd voices
Crying out of the timid future,
Where now is paradise, the hope foresworn,
That could have been, had the heart stretched to hold it?
Where now lost Eden? Behind locked eyelids only
Glimmering a moment in the trance of love,
Recalled for a moment during the truce of music—
The hyssop sponge tendered in mercy
To the parched spirit, fretful in its torment—
Temporary assuagement. The tune Time plays
Grows harder to dance to now. Man's cleverness
Outwits itself; while round the watchful planet
The shark-nosed bombers wait to be unsheathed,
And terror needles the world heartbreak.

Evening Contemplation II

Over the meadow-land
Where I so often have watched them,
To an ancient sound of the sea
Heavy upon this coast,
The summer stars look down—
A part of them, yet separate,
Singled by consciousness,
I stand and survey them here.
Deneb, Vega, Altair,
Hang high in the pure vault,
Trembling, and far below them
Venus, a fiery bloom
Fallen from the bough of heaven,
The great galactic vine,
Is glowing deep in the west.
Now from the fields unnumbered
Small creatures lift their hymn,
Cricket and grasshopper
Welcome with shrill noise
The illustrious presences,
They are here, they are here, they are here,
The glory that dwells in darkness
Has visited earth once more.
The heavens preserve their secret,
From the rim of the huge vault
To the high sidereal arches
No sound. Perpetual silence!
Infinite peace! But oh,

Universe of hushed light,
That peace will not deceive me;
Horrible process, divine
Agony and splendor,
Too well I know your ways,
Their grandeur and their vileness:
The tenderness, the brute
Bestiality, the bloody
Pattern of things on earth,
The fangs that rend the living
Body, the cruel delight,
The terror and the torment,
I know them—and in the heavens
Your dread and violent way
From nebula to system,
The throes of your vast elation,
Convulsions, whirlwinds of stars,
Fierce galaxies without number,
Staining the virgin darkness.
Also, the high sublime
Way of your lonely dreaming
In arches of ordered color
Where the rainbow curves the light
Over a trailing cloud,
The sorrow of void sea-spaces,
And the bolt of bright flame,
And the listening heart of a mother—
I know them, O divine truth,
Who stand here, for a moment
Permitted while the red blood

In leaping faithfulness flushes
Body and brain with the old
Incomparable elixir—
Permitted so, for a time,
To be aware of you now,
To worship and to adore you,
Holy substance of things,
From which the body of love
Is fashioned, the oceanic
Rhythm, the wild Spring rain,
And the music of a Beethoven,
And of which I too am part
Forever. Oh, consoling
Thought, forever, forever
One with your timeless being,
More fully even than now,
When the temporal separation
Through consciousness shall be ended,
That consciousness in which
So briefly you were mirrored,
O sole and perfect truth,
When I lie down to mix
With your beauty in the darkness,
When I drag your glory down,
With me, into the grave.

Summer Night

The soft sound that leaves make in summer night,
When a warm wind is mild among the boughs,
Will wake us from our sleep, fitful and light,
Toward morning, as we drowse.

The heart, that has been sorrowful of late,
Stirs at that tender sound, and listens then
For some far-off, lost thing—but cannot wait,
Soon sunken in dream again.

A Walk with the Wind

Sea-wind, you comradely
Sharer in my delight,
By this autumnal sea,
In slant October light,
What word have you for me?

With thunder-throated roar
The lions of the surf
Descend upon the shore,
The leaping breakers curve
Downward in death once more.

But you, your word is of
Realms far beyond their foam,
Waters where sea-birds rove
The sea, which is your home,
The sea, the mother of love.

Sea-odors, salt and strange,
You bring out of the vast
Blue solitudes you range,
And memories out of the past,
Safe now from chance and change—

Memories of a still face
Where love has sealed the eyes,
The as-if-listening face,
Hushed lips and parted thighs
Of love's divine embrace.

To him you walk with here
Your voice, O sea-wind, brings
Lost hours very near,
Such unforgotten things
You speak into his ear.

From shifting light and cloud
The great sea, like a glass
Over which heaven is bowed,
Takes color as they pass—
Clear light or shadow of cloud.

Pale green along the sky,
But, on the waste between,
Color and darkness vie:
Sea-blue, or somber green
Where the cloud-shadows lie.

Pure sea, pure sky, pure sand,
Unviolated space
Flawless on either hand,
And barren dunes that face
Seaward, a lonely land.

Waters by heaven rimmed,
Beaches where as a boy
I strode, as eager-limbed
Today as then—oh, joy
Still with me, still undimmed!

To watch the sea-gull rest
On the wind's long incline
His ever-mounting breast
The heart leaps up in mine,
I know myself for blessed.

Watching the gulls, the sea,
But from another shore,
There walks a man like me
Who, for some future war,
Is named the enemy.

He scans the waters there,
Out to the farthest rim;
He thinks of me somewhere
Perhaps, as I of him,
The enemy striding there.

Sea-wind, wild and fleeting,
Go, give that other one,
In lieu of other meeting,
This word, my benison:
Tell him all men are one,
Bring him a brother's greeting.